CONTINUUM
MUSIC BY JOHN MAYER

CONTENTS

This book was approved by John Mayer

Piano/vocal arrangements by John Nicholas

Cherry Lane Music Company
Director of Publications/Project Editor: Mark Phillips
Manager of Publications: Gabrielle Fastman

ISBN-13: 978-1-57560-945-4
ISBN-10: 1-57560-945-2

Visit our website at www.cherrylane.com

JOHN MAYER CONTINUUM

"With any trilogy," says John Mayer, "the third in the series blows it open."

On *Continuum* the singer/songwriter/ guitar slinger meets that challenge head-on. Mayer's third studio album follows the multi-platinum *Room for Squares* (2001) and *Heavier Things* (2003) and marks his first turn as producer. It is his most soulful, cohesive collection yet and he says it's no accident that this project is where all of his efforts, his potential, and his disparate influences fully come together.

"The night I was recognized for 'Daughters' at the Grammys was the night this record started," he says. "I knew I had bought the time to learn everything I needed before I started this one. *Continuum* is not a shot in the dark, it's not a guesstimation. This is the first endeavor in my entire life, music or otherwise, that I did not cop out on for a second."

The last few years have seen Mayer maintaining a frantic pace. In addition to his own writing, recording, and touring, he has collaborated with icons and contemporaries alike—Eric Clapton, B.B. King, Buddy Guy, and Herbie Hancock, as well as Kanye West, the Dixie Chicks, and Alicia Keys. In doing so, Mayer says his own interests have grown and his perspectives have expanded. Mayer also credits his collaboration with Steve Jordan and Pino Palladino (collectively known as the John Mayer Trio) and the intimate-venue tour that produced the 2005 live album *Try!* with helping to recalibrate his musical priorities. "As a songwriter, the Trio helped me focus on being more raw," he says. "As a guitar player, it helped me get a lot out of my system. If it weren't for the Trio, *Continuum* would have been less accessible. It let me settle up with my needs as a musician, and get to a point somewhere between the Trio record and *Room for Squares*—and that's a really good place to be."

While the Trio tour showcased Mayer's blazing fretwork, he says he learned lessons from those shows about restraint. "When I made my first record, there was no trust in space because it was all me; everything was just on those six strings," he says. "With Steve and Pino it was all about space, using a whole different palette. When your tone is good on the guitar, you need, like, four notes. The more concise and right you have it, the less you need around it." One listen to such spare, carefully crafted songs as "Slow Dancing in a Burning Room" or "I Don't Trust Myself (With Loving You)" instantly reveals this new approach.

Mayer points to one song in particular as the turning point for *Continuum.* "I wrote 'Gravity' last summer, and it changed everything," he says. "You talk less when you trust that people understand you. 'Gravity' had to be sparse. And when I listened to it for the first time, holding back, it was a whole new game. That might be the most important song I ever wrote."

Armed with this outlook, Mayer knew *Continuum* would tackle larger ideas than those that defined his previous albums. "A big challenge was writing about big themes," he says. "I'm not a better writer in terms of sitting down in front of a pad, but I'm better in terms of receiving inspiration and converting it into something 'real' quicker. I'm better equipped to deal with those moments."

The hard-hitting "Belief" tackles an infinitely complex subject. Over a slinky, hypnotic guitar groove, he sings, "We're never gonna win the world, we're never gonna stop the war/We're never gonna beat this if belief is what we're fighting for," questioning the power and the limitations of faith and convictions. "It's an intellectual landmine—how do you write a song about what people believe without impugning their beliefs?" he asks. "I wanted

to get right next to people's beliefs and look at them without threatening them. It's tricky. You only get x number of syllables and you have to write something you can defend."

With "Waiting on the World to Change," Mayer shot for something even more ambitious— something like an attempt to explain his generation's attitudes about politics. "It's meant to shed a little light on inactivity and inaction," he says, "because I don't believe that inaction is a lack of interest. I think inaction is preservation—nobody wants to get involved in a debate in which the rules and facts will change so that they'll lose. So we end up with this other option, which is, I guess we'll just have to wait for things to get better.

Continuum also includes the first cover Mayer has put on an album, his version of "Bold As Love" by the incomparable Jimi Hendrix. "To me, it's the quintessential Jimi Hendrix song," says Mayer. "The sensitivity, the imagery, the power. I also think the third record is the time when you challenge everybody. It's your throw-down. I like inviting the challenge of, Should this guy even touch Hendrix's music? To which I answer, Well, everybody should. Why not?"

Ultimately, *Continuum* represents maturity, both musically and thematically, for John Mayer—a concept that he wasn't comfortable with until now. "A lot of these songs are about coming to terms with getting older," he says. "My generation was never told we were going to get older. We thought we were going to hear our names on *Romper Room* for the rest of our lives. For a long time, I was really upset about getting older, worried that things were just going to level out. But then I realized that everyone around me was getting older at the same time. We're all fighting it together, and we're always going to be those kids, the first really emotionally aware generation. When I realized that, I could relax about it a little bit. And I thought that maybe I can be the guy to sing about it."

Waiting on the World to Change

Words and Music by
John Mayer

Moderately

Me and all my friends, ___ we're all ___ mis - un - der - stood. ___ They
if we had the pow - er to bring our neigh - bors home ___ from war, ___ they would have

say we stand for noth - ing and ___ there's no way we ev - er could. Now we see
nev - er missed a Christ - mas; ___ no more rib - bons on their door. And when you

4

ev - 'ry - thing that's go - ing wrong _ with the world and those _ who lead it. We just
trust your tel - e - vi - sion, what you get is what _ you got. 'Cause when they

To Coda I

feel like we don't have _ the means _ to rise a - bove _ and beat it. So we keep
own the in - for - ma - tion, oh, _ they can

wait - ing (wait - ing), _ wait - ing on the world _ to change. We keep on

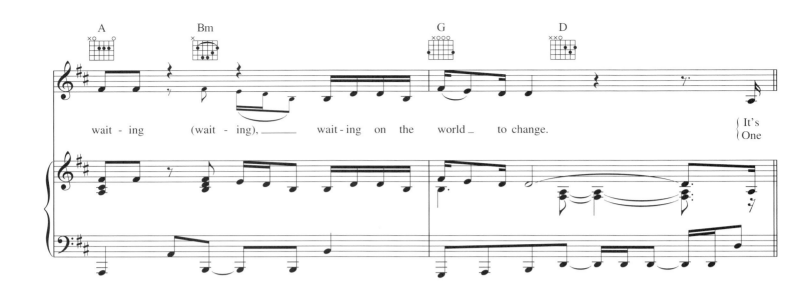

wait-ing (wait-ing), ____ wait-ing on the world _ to change. {It's
{One

hard to beat _ the sys-tem when we're stand-ing at ___ a dis-tance. So we keep)
day our gen-er-a-tion is gon-na rule the pop-u-la-tion. So we keep on)

To Coda II   *D.S. al Coda I*

wait-ing (wait-ing), ____ wait-ing on the world _ to change. Now,

world __ to change.

D.S.S. al Coda II

And we're still

I Don't Trust Myself
(With Loving You)

Words and Music by
John Mayer

No, I'm

_____ be - fore _____ I let you in - side. _____

_____ you back _____ all o - ver a - gain. _____ (I don't real - ly un - der - stand.)

Hold on to what - ev - er you find, ba - by.

Hold on to what - ev - er will get you _____ through.

14

Belief

Words and Music by
John Mayer

Moderately

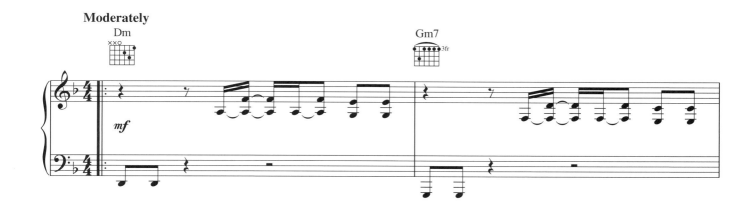

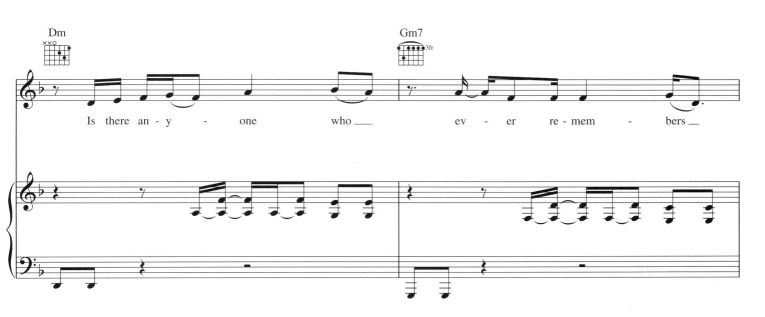

Is there an-y - one who ___ ev - er re-mem - bers ___

changing their mind from the paint on a sign.

Is there anyone who really recalls ever break-

ing rank at all for something someone yelled real loud one time.

Oh, ev'ryone believes

Be - lief ___ is a beau - ti - ful ar - mor, but makes ___ for the heav - i - est sword. ___

Like punch - ing un - der wa - ter, you nev - er can hit who you're try - ing for. ___

Some need the ex - hi - bi - tion, some have to know ___ they tried. ___

It's the chem-i-cal weap-on for the war___ that's rag-ing on___ in - side.___

Instrumental...

Oh, ev-'ry-one___ be - lieves,___

from emp-ti - ness___ to ev-'ry - thing.

Oh, ev-'ry-one___ be - lieves,___

and no one's go - ing qui - et - ly.

...Instrumental ends

We're nev - er gon - na win the world. __ We're nev - er gon - na stop the war. __

To Coda

We're nev - er gon - na beat this if __ be - lief __ is what __ we're fight - ing for. __

D.S. (with repeat) al Coda

Is there an-y - one   who can re-mem - ber,   ev - er sur-ren - der,   with their life   on   the line?   Da   da da da   da da   da   da da da   da

Gravity

Words and Music by
John Mayer

and grav-i-ty ___ wants to bring me down.

Oh, I'll nev-er know what makes this man,
Oh, twice as much twice as good

with all the love that his heart can stand,
and can't sus-tain like one-half could.

It's want-ing more ___ dream of ways ___ to that's gon-na

Coda

Woh, woh. ___ Grav - i - ty, ___ stay the hell a - way from ___ me. ___

Woh, woh. ___ Grav - i - ty ___ has tak - en bet - ter men ___ than ___ me. ___

28

The Heart of Life

Words and Music by
John Mayer

Moderately, in 2

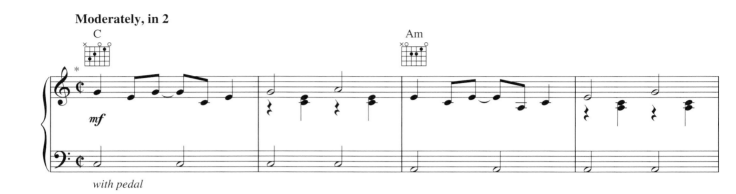

with pedal

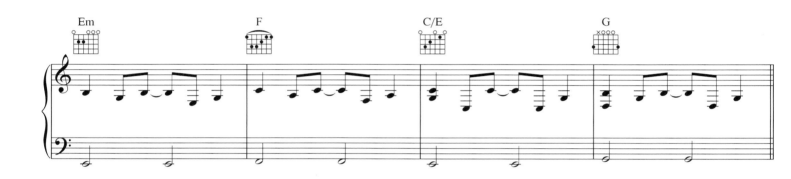

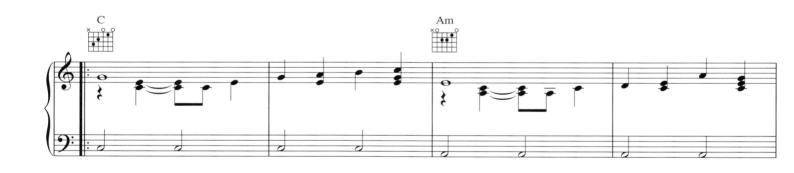

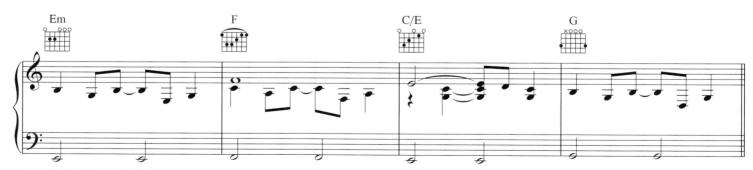

*Recorded a half step higher.

Pain throws _ your heart to _ the ground.

Love turns _ the whole thing _ a - round.

No, it _ won't all go _ the way it should, but I

know _ the heart of life _ is good.

Vultures

Words and Music by
John Mayer, Pino Paladino
and Steven Jordan

How will I hold my head to keep from go-ing un - der? Down to the wi - re.

I want-ed wa-ter but I'll walk through the fi - re. If this is what it takes to

take me e-ven high-er, then I'll come through like I do when the world keeps

test-ing me, test-ing me, test-ing me.

They've nev - er gone __ this long ____ with - out a kill __ be - fore. ____

Coda I

Amaj9

F#m11

F#m11

Wheels up, I got to leave this eve - ning.

I can't seem to shake these vul - tures off of my ___ trail. ___

Pow - er is ___ made ___ by pow - er be - ing tak - en.

D.S. al Coda II

So I keep on run - ning to pro - tect my sit - u - a - tion.

Coda II

Amaj9

test - ing me, test - ing me.   Whoo, ___

whoo.

What __ you gon - na do a - bout __ it? What __ you gon - na do a - bout __ it?

What __ you gon - na do a - bout it?

Repeat and fade

Stop This Train

Words and Music by
John Mayer and Pino Palladino

So scared of get - ting old - er; I'm on - ly good __ at be - ing young. __

So I play the num - bers game __ to find a way __ to say __ that life has

Slow Dancing in a Burning Room

Words and Music by
John Mayer

silly little mo - ment. It's not the storm be - fore _ the calm. _ This is the
one you al - ways dreamed of. You were the one I tried _ to draw. _ How dare you

deep and dy - ing breath of this love that we've been work - ing on. _____ Can't seem to
say it's noth - ing to me? Ba - by, you're the on - ly light _ I ev - er saw. _ I'll make the

Play 1st time only

hold you like I want to so I can feel you in ____ my arms. _ No bod - y's
most of all the sad - ness. You'll be a

gon - na come and save you. We pulled too man - y false ____ a - larms. We're go - ing _

50

Play 2nd time only

bitch be-cause __ you can. __ You'll try to hit me just to hurt me so you leave me feel-ing dirt-y, 'cause you

can't un-der-stand. We're go - ing __ down, __ and you can

see it, too. __ We're go - ing __ down, __ and you

know that we're doomed. __ My dear, __ we're slow danc-ing in a

burn - ing room. _

I was the

Go

cry a - bout _ it, why don't you?

Go

My dear, _ we're slow danc-ing in a burn - ing room. _

52

Bold As Love

Words and Music by
Jimi Hendrix

*Guitarists: Tune down a half step.

I'm bold, ___ I'm bold as love, _____ yeah. ___

Dreaming with a Broken Heart

Words and Music by
John Mayer

Now, do I have to
fall a - sleep _ with ros - es in my hand? _____
Do I have to

won't, __ 'cause you're gone, gone, gone, gone, gone.

When you're dream - ing with __ a bro - ken heart, __

the wak - ing up is the hard - est part. __

In Repair

Words and Music by
John Mayer and Charlie Hunter

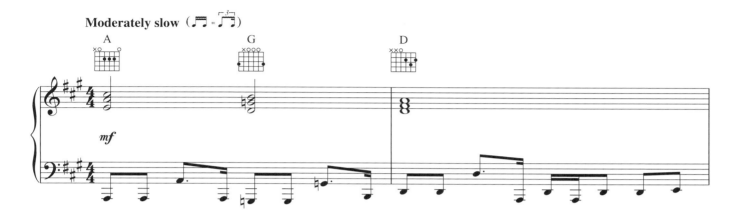

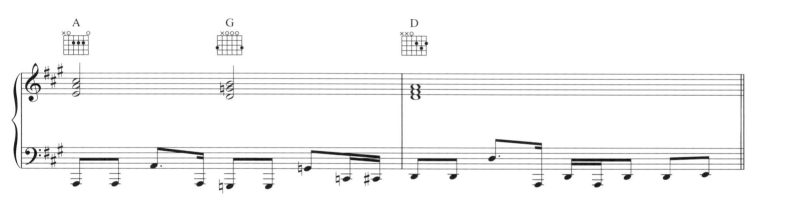

Too man - y shad - ows in ____ my room.
Stood on the cor - ner for ____ a while
And now I'm walk - ing in ____ the park,

Too man-y ho - urs in this mid - night.
to wait for the wind to blow down on _____ me,
and all of the birds, they dance be - low _____ me.

Too man-y cor - ners in my ___ mind.
hop-ing it takes with it ___ my old ways
May - be when things turn green a - gain,

So much to do to set my heart _____ right.)
and brings some brand - new luck up - on _____ me.
it will be good to say you know _____ me.

70

I'm Gonna Find Another You

Words and Music by
John Mayer

More Great Piano/Vocal Books

FROM CHERRY LANE

For a complete listing of Cherry Lane titles available,
including contents listings, please visit our web site at

www.cherrylane.com

02500343 Almost Famous $14.95
02502171 The Best of Boston $17.95
02500672 Black Eyed Peas – Elephunk . . . $17.95
02500665 Sammy Cahn Songbook $24.95
02500144 Mary Chapin Carpenter –
       Party Doll & Other Favorites . . $16.95
02502163 Mary Chapin Carpenter –
       Stones in the Road $17.95
02502165 John Denver Anthology –
       Revised $22.95
02502227 John Denver –
       A Celebration of Life $14.95
02500002 John Denver Christmas $14.95
02502166 John Denver's Greatest Hits $17.95
02502151 John Denver – A Legacy
       in Song (Softcover) $24.95
02502152 John Denver – A Legacy
       in Song (Hardcover) $34.95
02500566 Poems, Prayers and Promises: The Art
       and Soul of John Denver $19.95
02500326 John Denver –
       The Wildlife Concert $17.95
02500501 John Denver and the Muppets:
       A Christmas Together $9.95
02509922 The Songs of Bob Dylan $29.95
02500586 Linda Eder – Broadway My Way $14.95
02500497 Linda Eder – Gold $14.95
02500396 Linda Eder –
       Christmas Stays the Same $17.95
02500175 Linda Eder –
       It's No Secret Anymore $14.95
02502209 Linda Eder – It's Time $17.95
02500630 Donald Fagen – 5 of the Best . . . $7.95
02500535 Erroll Garner Anthology $19.95
02500270 Gilbert & Sullivan for Easy Piano $12.95
02500318 Gladiator $12.95
02500273 Gold & Glory:
       The Road to El Dorado $16.95
02502126 Best of Guns N' Roses $17.95
02502072 Guns N' Roses – Selections from
       Use Your Illusion I and II $17.95
02500014 Sir Roland Hanna Collection . . . $19.95
02500352 Hanson – This Time Around . . . $16.95
02502134 Best of Lenny Kravitz $12.95
02500012 Lenny Kravitz – 5 . . . . $16.95
02500381 Lenny Kravitz – Greatest Hits . . . $14.95
02503701 Man of La Mancha $10.95

02500693 Dave Matthews – Some Devil . . . $16.95
02500555 Dave Matthews Band –
       Busted Stuff $16.95
02500003 Dave Matthews Band – Before
       These Crowded Streets $17.95
02502199 Dave Matthews Band – Crash . . $17.95
02500390 Dave Matthews Band –
       Everyday $14.95
02500493 Dave Matthews Band – Live in Chicago
       12/19/98 at the United Center . $14.95
02502192 Dave Matthews Band – Under
       the Table and Dreaming $17.95
02500681 John Mayer – Heavier Things . . $16.95
02500563 John Mayer – Room for Squares $16.95
02500081 Natalie Merchant – Ophelia $14.95
02500423 Natalie Merchant – Tigerlily . . . $14.95
02502895 Nine $17.95
02500425 Time and Love: The Art and
       Soul of Laura Nyro $19.95
02502204 The Best of Metallica $17.95
02500407 O-Town $14.95
02500010 Tom Paxton – The Honor
       of Your Company $17.95
02507962 Peter, Paul & Mary –
       Holiday Concert $17.95
02500145 Pokemon 2.B.A. Master $12.95
02500026 The Prince of Egypt $16.95
02500660 Best of Bonnie Raitt $17.95
02502189 The Bonnie Raitt Collection . . . $22.95
02502230 Bonnie Raitt – Fundamental . . . $17.95
02502139 Bonnie Raitt –
       Longing in Their Hearts $16.95
02502088 Bonnie Raitt – Luck of the Draw $14.95
02507958 Bonnie Raitt – Nick of Time . . . $14.95
02502190 Bonnie Raitt – Road Tested $24.95
02502218 Kenny Rogers – The Gift $16.95
02500072 Saving Private Ryan $14.95
02500197 SHeDAISY –
       The Whole SHeBANG $14.95
02500414 Shrek $14.95
02500536 Spirit – Stallion of the Cimarron $16.95
02500166 Steely Dan – Anthology $17.95
02500622 Steely Dan –
       Everything Must Go $14.95
02500284 Steely Dan –
       Two Against Nature $14.95
02500165 Best of Steely Dan $14.95

02500344 Billy Strayhorn:
       An American Master $17.95
02502132 Barbra Streisand –
       Back to Broadway $19.95
02500515 Barbra Streisand –
       Christmas Memories $16.95
02507969 Barbra Streisand – A Collection:
       Greatest Hits and More $17.95
02502164 Barbra Streisand – The Concert $22.95
02500550 Essential Barbra Streisand $24.95
02502228 Barbra Streisand –
       Higher Ground $16.95
02500196 Barbra Streisand –
       A Love Like Ours $16.95
02500280 Barbra Streisand – Timeless . . . $19.95
02503617 John Tesh – Avalon $15.95
02502178 The John Tesh Collection $17.95
02503623 John Tesh – A Family Christmas $15.95
02505511 John Tesh –
       Favorites for Easy Piano $12.95
02503630 John Tesh – Grand Passion $16.95
02500124 John Tesh – One World $14.95
02500307 John Tesh – Pure Movies 2 . . . . $16.95
02500565 Thoroughly Modern Millie $17.95
02500576 Toto – 5 of the Best $7.95
02502175 Tower of Power –
       Silver Anniversary $17.95
02502198 The "Weird Al" Yankovic
       Anthology $17.95
02502217 Trisha Yearwood –
       A Collection of Hits $16.95
02500334 Maury Yeston – December Songs $17.95
02502225 The Maury Yeston Songbook . . . $19.95

See your local music dealer or contact:

CHERRY LANE
MUSIC COMPANY
6 East 32nd Street, New York, NY 10016

Quality in Printed Music

EXCLUSIVELY DISTRIBUTED BY

HAL•LEONARD®
CORPORATION
7777 W. BLUEMOUND RD. P.O. BOX 13819 MILWAUKEE, WI 53213

Prices, contents and availability subject to change without notice.

0404

great songs series

Cherry Lane Music is proud to present this legendary series which has delighted players and performers for generations.

Great Songs of the Fifties

The latest release in Cherry Lane's acclaimed Great Songs series, this songbook presents 51 musical memories from the fabulous '50s! Features rock, pop, country, Broadway and movie tunes, including: All Shook Up • At the Hop • Blue Suede Shoes • Dream Lover • Fly Me to the Moon • Kansas City • Love Me Tender • Misty • Peggy Sue • Rock Around the Clock • Sea of Love • Sixteen Tons • Take the "A" Train • Wonderful! Wonderful! • and more. Includes an introduction by award-winning journalist Bruce Pollock.

_____02500323 P/V/G.............................$16.95

Great Songs of the Sixties, Vol. 1 – Revised Edition

The newly updated version of this classic book includes 80 faves from the 1960s: Angel of the Morning • Bridge over Troubled Water • Cabaret • Different Drum • Do You Believe in Magic • Eve of Destruction • Georgy Girl • It Was a Very Good Year • Monday, Monday • People • Spinning Wheel • Walk on By • and more.

_____02509902 P/V/G.............................$19.95

Great Songs of the Sixties, Vol. 2 – Revised Edition

61 more 60s hits: And When I Die • California Dreamin' • Crying • The 59th Street Bridge Song (Feelin' Groovy) • For Once in My Life • Honey • Little Green Apples • MacArthur Park • Me and Bobby McGee • Nowhere Man • Piece of My Heart • Sugar, Sugar • You Made Me So Very Happy • and more.

_____02509904 P/V/G.............................$19.95

Great Songs of the Seventies – Revised Edition

This super collection of 70 big hits from the '70s includes: After the Love Has Gone • Afternoon Delight • Annie's Song • Band on the Run • Cold as Ice • FM • Imagine • It's Too Late • Layla • Let It Be • Maggie May • Piano Man • Shelter from the Storm • Superstar • Sweet Baby James • Time in a Bottle • The Way We Were • more!

_____02509917 P/V/G.............................$19.95

Prices, contents, and availability subject to change without notice.

Great Songs of the Seventies – Volume 2

Features 58 outstanding '70s songs in rock, pop, country, Broadway and movie genres: American Woman • Baby, I'm-A Want You • Day by Day • Do That to Me One More Time • Dog & Butterfly • Don't Cry Out Loud • Dreamboat Annie • Follow Me • Get Closer • Grease • Heard It in a Love Song • I'll Be There • It's a Heartache • The Loco-Motion • My Eyes Adored You • New Kid in Town • Night Fever • On and On • Sing • Summer Breeze • Tonight's the Night • We Are the Champions • Y.M.C.A. • and more. Includes articles by Cherry Lane Music Company founder Milt Okun, and award-winning music journalist Bruce Pollock.

_____02500322 P/V/G.............................$19.95

Great Songs of the Eighties – Revised Edition

This newly revised edition features 50 songs in rock, pop & country styles, plus hits from Broadway and the movies! Songs: Almost Paradise • Angel of the Morning • Do You Really Want to Hurt Me • Endless Love • Flashdance...What a Feeling • Guilty • Hungry Eyes • (Just Like) Starting Over • Let Love Rule • Missing You • Patience • Through the Years • Time After Time • Total Eclipse of the Heart • and more.

_____02502125 P/V/G.............................$18.95

Great Songs of the Nineties

This terrific collection features 48 big hits in many styles. Includes: Achy Breaky Heart • Beautiful in My Eyes • Believe • Black Hole Sun • Black Velvet • Blaze of Glory • Building a Mystery • Crash into Me • Fields of Gold • From a Distance • Glycerine • Here and Now • Hold My Hand • I'll Make Love to You • Ironic • Linger • My Heart Will Go On • Waterfalls • Wonderwall • and more.

_____02500040 P/V/G.............................$16.95

Great Songs of the Pop Era

Over 50 hits from the pop era, including: Amazed • Annie's Song • Ebony and Ivory • Every Breath You Take • Hey Nineteen • I Want to Know What Love Is • I'm Every Woman • Just the Two of Us • Leaving on a Jet Plane • My Cherie Amour • Raindrops Keep Fallin' on My Head • Rocky Mountain High • This Is the Moment • Time After Time • (I've Had) the Time of My Life • What a Wonderful World • and more!

_____02500043 Easy Piano $16.95

CHERRY LANE MUSIC COMPANY
6 East 32nd Street, New York, NY 10016
Quality in Printed Music
Visit Cherry Lane on the Internet at
www.cherrylane.com

EXCLUSIVELY DISTRIBUTED BY

HAL•LEONARD® CORPORATION
7777 W. BLUEMOUND RD. P.O.BOX 13819 MILWAUKEE, WI 53213

0402